America What A Country - What A Joke!

The Government of Master of Deception

by

Cyrus Yassai

authorHOUSE™

1663 LIBERTY DRIVE, SUITE 200
BLOOMINGTON, INDIANA 47403
(800) 839-8640
WWW.AUTHORHOUSE.COM

First published by AuthorHouse 02/17/05

ISBN: 1-4208-2340-X (sc)

Printed in the United States of America
Bloomington, Indiana

This book is printed on acid-free paper.

Five years into the 21st Century, Americans have been prosperous in making enemies among millions of people around the World who have implicitly and explicitly expressed their hate toward the bully American Government and its' sheep allies.

Currently there are at least three truly terrorist Governments, in order they are: the United State of America, the Government of Israel and the fanatic pseudo-religious Government of Iran's mullas.

Bill of Rights
(Article 1)
Freedom of speech and press

It is a shame to know how the Bush's Administration's notion of deception by spreading the seeds of terror among naive American leymen and leywomen overwhlmed and overpowered them to be freightened enough not to look into the crime the U.S. Government has done against humanity first in Afganistan and then in Iraq. In Iran the Government using tools such as accusation, oppression and suppression stifles opponents - in America the Government commits same crime by terrorizing people of imaginary non-existing terrorism in the name of national security to achieve its' Satanic plots. At the mercy! of Master of deception George Bush (both father and son) the American Government has proven to be the most successful criminal and terrorist entity in the World in recent years. If terrorism means (per Webster's Dictionary) systematic use of terror as a means of keeping or gaining control of a government, then look for it in the White House, the core of can of warms.

Preface

To all those who leave their country voluntarily looking for a better life to fill up their desire of self esteem, to find political asylum, to reach what is known as freedom, in search of a decent job to feed the family, and to make all their dreams come true.

A great number of foreigners moving to U.S.A. are in the wrong direction, the direction to U.S.A. Where the flashy life takes it's toll everyday in the number of dozens in large cities and even small towns; they are not unaffected by crime, a destructive social phenomenon, sickening and typical of Western nations, in particular, eating America since it began to label itself as civilized. It appears that the Government tends to hide it's head into sands by pretending lack of existence of crime, after all a criminal society cannot be a civilized one. Because these two, for the obvious reason, contradict each other, in other words, you cannot be both civilized and criminal at the same time and of course it is humiliating to admit being criminal which the U.S. Government has opted out to be labeled as such, it decided to give the false name of high society to itself. But what is a high society? If technology, invention, discovery and development are good tools to increase welfare and sophistication for it's citizens in the society in which they live, then, the same tools must help the Government authorities to tackle themselves in confronting the law breakers in such a better way resulting in diminishing number of crime and criminals. But what we see is not what we are supposed to get according to our analogy of the reality of what truly exists. Some thirty years ago the number of slain victims of crime was about ten thousand a year. Today it is about forty thousand a year taking into consideration the population has not increased with the same pace as crime.

The day the U.S. Government passed the most notorious and shameful law of letting people carry guns the ground for a savage society was planned. This is not the Swiss society, this is America.!

A note to the readers

Most of the events mentioned in this book are the author's personal experiences. Therefore, denial of those is inconsequential. Since one's experience is the best teacher and proof to shed light on what has happened (practice makes it perfect), the author dares to challenge any objection to the contents of this book. Nobody can manipulate the truth, the truth will always be there no matter what we do (we may cover it up but it's there). Some of the incidents in the book are facts and some others are trends. When the same thing happens at times and or similar to those has taken place quite many times or there are indications or connections that similar situations may occur in future, then, we have to accept it and think of it as a trend which has happened and that possibly can happen again. And I have to conclude that since I have been exposed to such bitter ordeals numerously, it makes sense to say many other people have gone thru similar situations as well.

John F. Kennedy said "Don't ask what your country can do for you, but ask what you can do for your country". My comment to Kennedy is that people are already doing the best thing for their country by having their tremendous

1

amount of tax money confiscated by the government; now it is the government 's duty to take advantage of that money to the best interests of the people.

America what a country!

Where having access to guns gives the best excuse to everybody to shoot at anybody who may give excuses to be shot at. Where if people did not have guns to defend themselves against the intruder, then, the intruder would not have a gun either to threaten in the first place. After all nobody would be allowed to have guns. So, the question arises that whether people be allowed to have guns or not to have guns. If allowed to have guns, then, chances are that the criminal or prospective criminal has a gun already so that he can be prepared for the unexpected. And in that case if the defendant has a gun, most likely the criminal would use it and so does the defendant. If the defendant does not poses a gun, then, he is about to be subdued and give the criminal what he wants. And of course this is a green light to every criminal to go on his man hunting spree. Now what if neither the criminal nor the crime victim has a gun? Odds are extremely slim that one or both due to unusual circumstances may be killed or even injured. Hence, equipping people with guns, as we see, is to nobody's advantage. The only useful application of carrying a gun seems to be a situation where the unarmed invader attacks while his victim is armed and ready to threaten and or use his weapon to deter the criminal or injure or kill him.

America what a country!

It only happens here in America where some lawyers write books about " Why law suits are good for America". As bad as it sounds it exists. And as long as there are people who claim usefulness of law suits, the American society will remain to be a highly aggressive, criminal, unsafe, insecure and dangerous.

The American people, in general, do not seem or do not act to notice the destructive effects of crime in their country. They grow up with it, they see it on television, in movies, hear about it on radio, they are smothered with it, courts shelter criminals, lawyers defend them, people achieve crime, tourists become their victims, police chase them, victims pay hefty price for them involuntarily and the Government does it sometimes and occasionally admits doing them.

3

The U.S. Government sometimes commits crime in the form of trying to assassinate an individual leader of another country(Fidel Castro for decades) and sometimes thru conspiracy with other governments against their own citizens (El Salvador, Guatemala, Columbia and more) and when those governments stop cooperating or shed light on the dirty nature of the American Government foreign policy, they are accused and or challenged in a dog fight effort to topple the leader of those countries (Noriega of Panama, Dr. Mohammad Mosaddegh of Iran and others). In the United States of America only fools believe in the honesty of the Government. If among everything the late, old and not very intelligent Khomeini of Iran said two things came out to be true, one was that the U.S. Embassy in Tehran was the nest of espionage and the second thing is that U.S. is the Great Satan. At least when it comes to relations with weak countries the U.S. foreign policy is no short of cruelty; on economic issues it exploits weak governments ignoring their human rights as long as it gets something out of those countries (Egypt, Turkey, Saudi Arabia, Israel, Iran, even when the Shah of Iran was in power), have had some of the worst human rights violations, despite all this U.S.A. has remained silent.

4

America what a country!

Where so much misconception, misperception, misinformation, derived from propaganda has fooled millions of poor, desperate, unprivileged, uneducated and unsophisticated people from, so to speak, Third World countries, where they gather to pursue and gain human rights as known to be on everybody's agenda. Some who were poor got rich, some who were rich got poor, some became victims of crime and carry the stigma of crime for the rest of their life. Children caught in the cross fire, businessmen shot at in their work place, drivers pulled out from their cars at gun point and tourists who lost their life forever; their sin was to tour some parts of the country. Their bodies became souvenirs for the family members!

America what a country!

A country where politicians believe if one murders another human being, he deserves to be executed (state of Texas is notorious for that), if he takes two human beings' life, he may be set free at the mercy of insufficient evidences (O.J. Simpson's case) where a big slap in the face of the justice and court system reiterated and proved well how vulnerable are those who believe in the accuracy, efficiency, true justice and fairness of the system they have been bragging about for so many years. Where if the murderers slay dozens of innocent people, they either take shelter under the cover of being the Government officials (the Waco massacre perpetrated by F.B.I. agents) or in the case of a foreign country like the U.S. puppet country of Israel, the Israel Government murderers are invited to a bargaining table (when Israel massacred several hundreds of Palestinians in their camp some thirty years ago). The Israelis are the people who have been crying for about half a century for the genocide Hitler did to them which made the World feel pity for them, now they are doing similar crime to the Palestinians whose land immorally and without the permission of its' real land owners has been taken away by a symbolic organization called The United Nations in 1948 which is supposed to bring dignity, and belief in pursuing happiness for all human beings. What a shame on U.N. It seems like happiness got materialized very well for the Israelis and just the opposite for the Palestinian people. It achieved well its purpose if planned to carry out misery for the Palestinians and a big piece of free land for the Israelis.

So much propaganda about democracy and human rights has been spilled out by the propaganda machines of

U.S.A. both he Government and the media (definitely the embedded ones, ABC, CBS, NBC, FOX and especially the notorious CNN) so little of it has been achieved. They club the World for being the leader in believing in human rights, but, human rights are raped in the prisons in this country as well as prisons out of the country controlled by U.S. such as Guantanamo of Cuba and Abughraib of baghdad, Iraq.

America what a country!

Where everything anybody has ever heard about crime does exists but to a larger dimension. Where if fighting crime the way it has been so far could work, by now after a century of battling it should have worked out. But, as we all see not only it has not worked but it has multiplied. It is said and it makes a very good sense that if you want to see what you have been doing so far has worked or or not, just look at the result. Therefore The only rational reason to be found is that the U.S. Government is not doing something rational to solve the crime dilemma. Where if one does not have safety and security, he or she does not have almost anything. This is the country where nothing means anything. Neither a car, home, money, education nor honesty and belief in ethics. Ethics is a tool in the hands of a bunch of wealthy aristocrats who are hypocrites against the poor to convince them to stick to those moral issues; the same moral issues these hypocrites do not care about. In other words; morals are good for the poor so that the wealthy can get wealthier than before and the poor get poorer. And if money means anything it is interdependent with politics; politics and money. Money turns politicians into big ones and then they feed themselves and the contributors with more money and or positions and contracts (Halliburton and bachtel are some examples). This is a never ending cycle. A typical American is raised to always desire for more money. When he sets his goal for a certain amount of money and eventually reaches there he does not stop there. And this never ending trend continues until he dies. He is born for money, has lived for money, and dies while striving for more money. So, money becomes the centerpiece of his life deprecating other values. That's why there are so many buisinesses in this country open 24 hours a day, 7 days a week. America does not sleep!

America what a country!

Where if one does assault on other people or steals somebody's property, he may go to prison for few weeks or months, But if he breaks in a house owned by a judge, he may be incarcerated for a year. Where if the criminal's parent or close relative happens to work for the court, the criminal can get away with punishment. Where a violating police officer is given plenty of chances to commit more crime under the cover of being a government agent. He may be brought to justice only after numerous complaints and or demonstrations by the victim's relatives or other complaining citizens take place who do see double standards and injustice in the way states and federal governments have handled the case in the first place. This is the country where there are millions of outcries against discrimination, police brutality, government atrocity, unjust justice system, injustice, and racial unfairness. Where in the Twenty First Century there is still controversies, disputes, and statistics about racism, people's origins and ethnicity, whether they are Hispanic, Middle Eastern, Black or White, Oriental or American Indians and possibly some other categories. Where constitution refuses to recognize immigrants' choice of ideology in Communism when applying for permanent residency and citizenship. What a shame! It appears that what is good for the goose is not good for the gander. The Government is ashamed to talk about it and disclose this, after all how having a political ideology is ok for the American people but not for the prospective American citizens. And if the applicants indicate that they believe in Communism, obviously the I.N.S. will refuse to give them residency or citizenship on top of everything else; it explicitly reveals that if the applicant's answer favors communism, he may not be eligible, which means he will not be for sure eligible. For the past few years some other weird and unjustifiable pretexts have been added to the blackmail list of I.N.S. for the applicants: things like D.U.I. ticket or even admitting it, ever used marijuana, being a drunkard, or even a traffic ticket, etc. In the taking an oath for citizenship ceremony they tell you that if you don't agree with the Government, you can speak out and show your opposition but practically people cannot do it, because the Government has created such an environment of intimidation and bias that new citizens do not feel comfortable (that's why one hardly can find foreigners among the demonstrators); secondly, when it comes to actually doing it, they are along with the rest of the protesters embarrassed, intimidated, barred and even hurt by the savage police force. Therefore, freedom in The United States of America is literally conditional. The condition is that either support the Government or shut up. While the American society is the number one nation in consuming drugs the applicant for Green Card and or citizenship must be penalized for the same unethical privileges. America is where justice is raped by those in charge of justice by giving full authority to the police force to search anybody for any reason, anytime, anywhere to keep innocent people in prison in the name of home security, and to imprison and torture those labeled perpetrators even if their crime has not been proven.

As bad as torture sounds it does exist in prisons in this country, both physical and psychological. This is the country where police shove more than one hundred human beings into a small room called jail, suitable for not more than twenty, holding them for two hours with no access to drinking water and bathroom and when you ask the officer for water he warns you to watch out because he is armed! How disgraceful. Where so much is said and done about diminishment of air pollution on gasoline operated engines but yet school busses, city busses, and big rigs run on diesel fuel create the maximum amount of pollution. All one can do to see how true that is is to look at the thick black smoke coming out of the exhaust pipes of these giant air pollutants. Where airplanes once invented out of necessity for travel speed and comfort have become games for air show watchers. Thousands cubic feet of oxygen is swallowed only during take off. To that one must add the number of planes times the duration spent in the air just for the sake of creating jubilance and catchall among the viewers who are unaware of their contribution to the calamity. On the other hand, same people pay the most expensive price for gasoline ever in the history of this country (as of now November 2004). Where freeways once copied from Germany at the end of World War Two by Eisenhower to bring speed, ease, and comfort now half a century later those freeways are not free anymore as put by Gray Davis, former Governor of California. In many parts of the country travelers especially truckers pay a hefty price to pass thru. And it is a common scene in large cities to see them jammed with traffic merging from all directions coming to a halt. Where frustration derived from getting stuck in traffic reflects its' side effects in the form of getting to work late, taking anger back to the family, arguments, fighting, drive- by shooting, mechanical problems, running out of gas, those who have to be at certain places at certain time otherwise they lose a lot (attending a court case), and police give a boost to the traffic jam by pulling someone to the side to give tickets, or block one lane because of too much and lengthy bureaucratic paper work while charging the public with a traffic ticket. Where truckers on a regular basis have to stop by weigh stations to be scrutinized, expounded, impounded, abused, and punished because the officer happened to wake up on the wrong side of the bed that day or simply because the officer was too bored to sit on his butts! Where it is not uncommon for the sake of a missing piece of paper truckers are barred to continue driving; every trucker has stories of abusiveness. Where the Government rips off truckers thousands of dollars every truck every year for different fees. Where truckers have become scapegoats in the name of public safety. Where when a highway patrol guides and refers you as a trucker to a nearby mechanic for the mechanical problem of the truck, chances are the nearby mechanic is his cousin or in-law. Where highway patrols look into your eyes and may tell you just opposite to what the law says and what is worse is that the judge who got educated and trained to follow the law to be fair and impartial makes the same violations as the highway patrols;even when you mention to the judge that per article #.......(whatever it applies) the officer made such a violation and as a result he must be punished, the judge (Mr. nice guy!) tells you that he will not do it.. Where many police officers and highway patrols act like scamps who treat people like slaves and, then, deny their own wrong doings. Across the country there are hundreds of recruited police officers who have had counts of previous violations and misconducts against citizens enough to be rejected for employment with other police department, surprisingly they got the job,in other words,police departments hire officers with criminal background. Where officers are rude enough to make citizens hate them and this can be one of the reasons why some of them get shot at. Where some police officers and or highway patrols do not mind to rape and murder easy victims both female and male (San Diego and New York).

America what a country!

Where at all cost the police department has made a commitment to support theoretically and practically the violating criminal officers until the case gets on the nerve of the society to the degree that they cannot take it anymore because of public outcry. The trend changes dramatically when a citizen commits a crime. In other words, a criminal citizen does not get the luxurious reprimand that an officer gets given he has committed same crime. This is where when a weigh station police officer pulls your truck to the side and guides you to a certain dirt road leading to wreckage of your vehicle 's axle, neither he nor the system accepts responsibility, as a result, you will not get compensated for the damage when you complain about it. Also it is here in U.S.A. where when the Department of Transportation audits you, the rude auditor calls you a liar, accuses you and treats you like a criminal. Upon receiving the report of the audit you may find out that he made a prejudiced untrue report in which you see quite few libels. And when you complain against him rendering documents of how wrong he is and that he made a biased forged report, the corrupt system ignores you, and stubbornly backs up the liar auditor.

This is the nation smart enough to let themselves get cheated on by the hyppocrite Federal Government when it comes to issues such as threat from another country. For so many years Ronald Reagan fooled The American people by saying "Russians are coming";at the end those Russians turned out to be Americans themselves. The criminal administration of George W. Bush The Junior has learned that the best way to get people's consent and approval of the Government satanic plans is to use rhetoric which touch citizens' emotions such as nationalism, home land security, terrorism, democracy, freedom, human rights, patriotism, and national interest (satanic verses). People who use the slogan of patriotism by saying" we support our troops" truly do not understand the real message of it. They acknowledge it without knowing what that means. What they may tell you would be something like that they agree with the Government to send troops to war, say Iraq. The true meaning and message of such imbalanced and hastened patriotism is the fact that they want the troops to go to war to kill other human beings and be killed. Since war is not same as having a party we have to conclude that these so to speak patriots want to see human agony on both sides while negligent of this bitter fact and dormant in their message while they post a big sign in front of their house saying "We support our troops".I do not see how it can be in the interest of the American people the notorious fact that the U.S. Government donates every year ten billion dollars of the American tax payers to Israel so that the terrorist Government of Israel continue terrorizing the Palestinian people, demolishing their homes, shooting them to death, holding them at gun point, arresting them, handcuffing them, restricting them in their own home land,incarcerating them for years, and what other crimes who knows.This is exactly the crimes U. S. has been doing in Iraq. What a shame! U.S. is the country defending human rights, clubbing the World for it and for democracy. America has failed its' mission times after times to condemn its' puppet Israel for human rights violations in Palestine. Instead of being straightforward and honest U.S.representative cowardly either does not show up in the Security Council or if it does it abuses its' power by vetoing. Over and over the

United Nations (wrongfully settled in U.S.) has condemned Israel for those violations, but what comes out at the end of the tunnel is only misery of the Palestinian people whom U.N. agreed to return their land back to them. In 1967 U.N. Security Council adopted Resolution 242 "the land for peace" formula, based on which Israel would withdraw from territories occupied by Israel which means Israel to withdraw from the Sinai Peninsula, the Golan Heights, the Gaza Strip, the West Bank of the Jordan River, and East Jerusalem. That would solve the plight once and for all. Israel has refused the conclusion of that Resolution and as a result never carried it out. Hence, The United Nations has become more a matter of plaything than reality for the hero nation of Palestine for whom my heart goes and I have highest respect. Israel is the tiny country which did not exist until 1948 by merit of U.N.. In 1949 Israel gained 50% increase in territory. If we follow this all the way to today, we can see that this eroding aggressive is becoming like epidemic bacteria. If Israel really wants peace, all it needs to do is to forfeit the occupied land and leave it to Palestinians. Israel cannot occupy (by force of course) the land and then complain why palestinians blow up Israelis. If it had not occupied the land in the first place, there would not be so much blood shed on both sides. One simply cannot attack another country, confiscate others' homeland, demolish their homes and when the victims defend themselves and fight back the aggressive attacker, call them terrorists..The truth is that the Government of Israel is the real terrorist and the palestinians are freedom fighters. One cannot get into water and not get wet. Israel wants to own the occupied land and does not want to pay a price for it's wrong doing. Amazingly, emotions run more hot in those who support the illegal action of Israel than those who oppose the occupation. More than 500 Israeli Army men and women have refused to join the rest of military to demolish homes and other structures in Palestine. That is a good lesson for Ariel Sharon and for Gorge Bush a supporter of Israel.

America is where there is no enforcement on behalf of the U.N. to punish U.S.A. for ignoring U.N. disapproval of Iraq war, no recourse or guaranty that U.N. decision is considered final no matter who violates when security council gives its' resolution. The best reason why people obey rules and laws in every country is not that people are noble, they are not, it is only because of enforcement; no enforcement equals no obedience. Rule of law is only a dream if not backed up by an enforcing factor. Who would enforce reprimand placed by U.N. on the uncooperating nations? The answer is either nobody(in the case of Israel) or if is done, it applies only towards countries unaffected by the double standardization of the countries influencing U.N. This weakness and inability of U.N. is well crystalized in the U.S. war on Iraq in 2003. Before the war the U.S. Government under the impression of getting approval from U.N. launched a huge number of army force to Kuwait to battle Iraq. At the same time acting like a rightful one way party it went to U.N. begging for approval for war. When U.N.opposed the plan The U.S. Government began to beat its' head against the wall, the undreamable got materialized. U.N. turned down U.S. request and said no to war just as millions of people around the World did. In a very desperate attempt the U.S. Government began to beg some, so to speak, friendly countries to join the war; again another failure for U.S.A.. So it went to war alone, carried the stigma of shame, found no weapon of mass destruction, no atomic bomb, no chemical weapons, but paid a hefty price, and lost its' face before the World(I doubt it had any). So, where is enforcement of U.N. when U.S. broke the rule and did not heed the decision made by the Security Council of U.N.? We do not see it, no one else does either. What happened to Israel terrorizing Palestinians with the help of its' terrorist boss The United States of America? Who gave Israel atomic bomb and or helped it get one or build one so that down the road to build over 200 nuclear heads simultaneously cowardly covering them up?. Who gave Israel the f-16 airplanes and other weapons of mass destruction? And on top of all these conspiracies, every year ten billion dollars of the American people many of them struggle to make it for living here at home goes to Israel without permission from tax payers. That's confiscation. And why does 't Mohammad Ibrahimi, Chief nuclear inspector of U.N. inspection Committee condemn and place sanction on Israel? If Israel pretends not to have atomic bomb, why put Venunu, the Moroccan-Israeli atomic scientist in prison for 18 long years for charges of revealing the atomic bomb information   ? Venunu would not have contributed in developing the bomb if he knew he was feeding the baby snake which would turn into a monsterous dragon later on.

America what a country!

They talk about freedom, government by people for people. But they intentionally have decided to hurt people wherever the skyrocketing profit of the rulers is at risk. That's why police shoot rubber bullets into the crowd in Oakland, California who were opposing waging war against Iraq, hurting a lawyer, a council woman, and others indiscriminately, trying to disperse demonstrations gathered in front of the Bachtel company in San Francisco-the company funding the greedy Bush's Administration war machine in return for profit from war or involvement of Halliburton, Dick Cheney's company in drilling oil and oil related fire extinguishing money laundry bonanza and etc. The vicious circle of Bush, Cheney, Rumsfield, Powell, their yes woman Condolisa Rice is stigma for which anybody who believes in humanity and philanthropic ideas of making this World a better place to live feels ashamed. One cannot by any humane standard murders thousands of innocent human beings in Afghanistan to capture Taliban and or Ben Laden. Even Taliban did not murder few thousand Afghans like Bush did. If Ben Laden killed close to three thousand human beings on September 11, 2001 and he is considered a terrorist, then, George Bush is a terrorist, too; he is even worse after all he is blaming Ben Laden for the crime he did, on the other hand, Bush himself commits the same crime for which he criticizes Ben Laden. Therefore, George W. Bush is a terrorist, too. He was cause for dropping bombs over people killing thousands and injuring another thousands. History will judge about the genocide of those men, women, and children who were victims of Bush's crime against humanity. He is good in one thing: turning Afghanistan into a bigger and worse rubble. Just as Bush's Administration fooled the American people for war in Afghanistan he tried it in Iraq where U.S.A. was bogged down both by lack of progress and by losing U.S.A. credibility before World. Where the tyrant's greed and selfishness prevailed over his logic and wisdom, American soldiers' lives do not mean much to him and to the American Government. We have seen this in Vietnam, Korean War, Iraq War, Afghanistan War, and Iraq War again. Seems like atrocity is inherited in the Bush's family. Father and son share their common interest of tyranny when it comes to unloading their weapon of mass destruction over other nations(2 Iraq wars)(Japan, Korea, Vietnam, Afghanistan, by Bush and others). Crime and punishment should work apparently, but it does not, at least not here.

Despite over fifty thousand American soldiers' lives were lost in Vietnam Nixon was not happy to withdraw, he resigned under pressure of public in huge opposition to his Water Gate scandal and continuance of war in which not only defeat was looming but it was obvious. In other words, losing so many lives did not mean anything to him; he simply had made his mind to satisfy his inner evil regardless of the outcome. Here is the logic for the United States of America 's wrong doing in Afghanistan following

September 11, 2001. When somebody commits a crime, let's say, here in U.S.A. by law, they cannot just put that person in prison and or execute him. Because first they need to have a reason or reasons to arrest the perpetrator. Then, within a certain period of time (statue of limitation) his crime must be evidenced by collected information. Then, his case goes to trial for conviction. If only then by the long tedious and costly due process the accused perpetrator is condemned of committing the crime, he will be punished. There are stories in F.B.I. files of law breakers whose crime was certain but due to lack of evidence they had to set the criminal free. This is how it works and must work. Any deviation from this is illegal and immoral. In the case of Afghanistan the U.S. Government without proving that Ben Laden was behind collapsing of the twin towers in New York jumped into conclusion and labeled him as the one who did it. Where is U.S.A. evidence proving he did it? They never could come up with one because they did not have any. Here we see what exists in governments ruled by Fascist regimes where the plaintiff, defense lawyer, and judge are all same, in this case it is the American Government. There was no Ben Laden to defend himself. There was no evidence proving that the crime was committed by him. Is this the justice they club the World for? Exodus of millions of Afghan men, women, children, the old, the young, the sick, the desperate and homeless going thru extreme fatigue, sleeplessness, unsanitary conditions, physical and moral torture, separation among family members and not knowing where they are or will be, whether they are alive or dead, where to settle, hunger, thirst, decease, and other calamities would bring tears into every human being's eyes who believes in humanity, human dignity, and survival. Where are human rights here as described by United Nation ? Obviously the George Bush's cabinet members are putting their heads (if they have any)into sands pretending the World will pass on their crimes against humanity.

America what a country!

Where capitalism in its' best savage form leaves a distant gap between the poor and the rich, where one may own a skyscraper and another human sheltering outside in cold winter in a carton box at the foot of the same building and sometimes kicked out of the area by police like a stray dog, where seeing a line of homeless humans in the dark dirty corners of slums is typical in large cities, where the most make up of the homeless as expected comes from minorities, where extreme contradiction exists between wealth and poverty, hunger and saturation, quantity in ownership of wealth and lack of that, quality of life and opposite side of it, where human misery in the richest country is a common scene in small sized towns as well as large cities. This is where the Government has found different ways of how to cheat on its' citizens by taking money from them for the services it provides(one of them is to see your money going down the drain in pre- emptive wars for nothing), where police officers exercise their talents of ripping off people by giving them hefty traffic tickets sometimes for nothing, simply because they are bored, where almost everybody knows the traffic police officers have been trained to reach the quotient to make the police department richer than it is, where laws only work to the benefit of the Government, laws such as seat belt, helmet, limitation on number of people on a car, not being allowed to accommodate in the back of a pick up truck(as if people are slaves who need the Government to be their master; people don't need the Government to cry for them in the name of public safety), prohibition of taking more than $ 10,000 cash out of the country even if it is one's own money, nobody is allowed to leave their car on the side of the freeway for over 4 hours at least here in California, nobody is allowed to enter a court without being scrutinized by the humiliating system of going thru the security device, where the idea of being as rich as possible is a novelty, where the poor does not count, where Government entities have become buisinesses rather than focussing on truly serving the public to their best possible interests, where D.M.V... does not mind to get rich at people's cost when they charge up to several hundred dollars for license plates stickers on pick up trucks claimed to have commercial bodies, where public pays a Hefty amount of tax money on tangible and intangible items.

America what a country!

Land of plenty of food, but no smell, taste or flavor, where fruits and vegetables are picked up too early and that's why they are not ripe and delicious, where almost everything is farm raised or green house effect, where the look on the outside always prevails the quality inside, where livestocks are stuffed with hormones and artificially fed, live poultry are sandwiched in the back of trucks like jews in the concentration camps and many die on route, where chickens are fed with artificial food to make their meat softer, where beef is dyed an artificial color in the stores to make it look good and fresh, where nearly all the fish on the market are farm raised, where there are sufficient evidence and rumors for one to be suspicious of the the Government to allow such policy of unnaturally raised animals whose meat consumption is notoriously known to result cancer, the # 1 killing decease in America. This is where cucumbers purchased at supermarkets taste like papers, tomatoes have no flavor, and cigarets carry chemicals. America is where the Government brags about what it does if those things bring positive results, but hides or at least tries to hide when outcomes are not favorable. Where if a criminal murders a government agent, the subject goes in the headline of the embedded media; but if an agent shoots a citizen to death, the agent is supported at any price by police department to avoid prosecution. They do everything they can to cover it up if not to come up with all kinds of made up reasons to free him and if that does not work because of public outcry and publicity, they try to give him the minimum punishment (cases of police brutality across the country is common). Likewise, In the country full of police officers with moral turpitude, if police do not find enough charges against their victims for incarceration, immediately fabrication of evidences and stories follow frisking the victim. This is the country where when police find your stolen car they call their business partner to rip you off, a certain tow truck company who may share the profits of ripping off the public with the police department, of course it is done in a covered action unknown to the public. Whereas they can call the owner of the stolen vehicle to take his car back they refuse to do so; if you ask them why they did not call you first, their answer is" we don't have to ". What a shame! This is where a typical police officer is considered to be rude and aggressive. One hardly comes across an officer with a smile on his face, Their eyes are always hidden behind sunglasses. This is the country where Americans are intelligent enough to create an atmosphere of fear, guns and murder, bloodshed, aggression, assault, battery, larceny, homicide, suicide, vandalism, graffiti, robbery, rape, stalking, theft, kidnapping, school shooting, drive-by shooting, and other side effects of a sick society. This is where dead human bodies are found everywhere, at their homes, in rivers, lakes, in the bushes, side of freeways, forests, inside car trunks, inside dumpsters, on the streets, and at their buisinesses. Forty thousand Americans are killed by other Americans every year in this country. This is where statistics for car accidents among states race against each other, drunk drivers take their toll in the thousands, hit and run is becoming more and more common scenes than ever, drive-by shooting the latest phenomenon to be added to other American innovations of killing each other. This is a nation very thirsty for blood with no end to all these violations. When these people make their way to the White House they continue doing same thing there; that's why we have had 2 George Bushes(creatives of 2 Iraq wars), Ronald Reagan (genius and founder of budget deficit), Nixon (wizard of Watergate scandal), Linden Johnson (the original launcher of Vietnam war), and so on. This is the country that does not mind to drop agent orange on enemy and on its' own soldiers for tryout and then deny it (in Vietnam), fools soldiers by calling them good soldiers and heroes but later refuse to take care of them when the war is over. Most of those who survived the Vietnam War became alcoholic, drug addict, depressed, jobless, skill-less, homeless, panhandlers, and suicide victims (we all have seen thousands of them at intersections and elsewhere across the country). The Desert Storm surviving soldiers complain about a mysterious decease derived from the war, but the Government tries to cover it up. When U.S. helicopters and airplanes fall down due to enemy fire, denial of the fact is very eminent. The Government claims its' helicopter failure is either because of mechanical problem or friendly fire. This is nature of the hypocrite capitalist government. Whenever they can lie to the World, they do it until they cannot hide it anymore. If they drop bombs on freedom fighters, its ok because the freedom fighters are supposedly terrorists and or insurgents. But if the enemy does same thing, again the enemy is terrorist and they are the bad guys and the U.S. soldiers are the good guys. Either way it should be always the enemy to be blamed, no matter how much Americans commit crime in the war; as if the devil of war gets its back only on opposite side and hence discriminates against U.S. enemy. This is how the U.S. Government justifies its' pretexts for exterminating over 100, 000 Iraqis(per a John Hopkin's University research) and over 8, 000 Afghans(a precise figure is not available). And who is that fool who believes that American soldiers' blood is redder than that of the enemy?.

America what a country!

Land of fruits without flavor, vegetables without smell, land of wealth and poverty, beauty and beast, justice and atrocity, fairness and callousness, religion and crime, rape and assault, black and white, discrimination and denial of it, hall of fame and hall of shame, land of foreigners and Americans, those who make it and those who fail it, land of job and joblessness, hard work and laziness, ideology and pragmatism, those who commit suicide and those who make every effort to survive at any cost, those who run their life to make it for living and those who run for their life at the cost of crime, land of rape and rapist, land of saturated prisons and over 2 million prisoners (a civilized society would not have prisoners), land of broken hearts, shattered marriages and families, land of abused, misused, and missing innocent children, land of foster parents and older people homes known as nursing homes, where one's life is not anymore noble and valuable (many of them are abused at the hands of the care takers), land of too many cars out of proportion, land of prostitution as common as it used to be though illegal by name, land of narcotics, narcotics sellers, narcotics buyers, and narcotics users, some of them ordinary citizens and some government officials like police officers themselves, land of farm raised animals for consumption, green house fruits and vegetables, land of all kinds of cancer, heart attack, malnutrition, obesity, land of "all you can eat smorgasbords "for the same price and nobody eats more than the top Government officials who swallow tax payers' hard earned money for personal use and campaign advertising when they run for office (Ronald Reagan especially was very good at it) or war arsenals, more than three hundred billion dollars budget deficit burden associated with the Government when Reagan was in power, that is power! Now George W. Bush the Texan cowboy warmonger is reviving it.

America what a country!

Where in large cities there are hundreds of war zones comprised of slums and ghettos where when one walks thru the streets of the poverty stricken areas, crime is felt in the air, insecurity and unsafety is easily touched, fear of assault and getting rubbed overwhelms and a feeling of fear and hate towards what potentially can take place in those areas warns you enough not to enter or if you do, expect to be a victim of crime, Where police cars carry with them stories of all kinds of perpetrators of law disobedience, be that misdemeanor, felony and or crime. Where in this cat and mouse chase between violators and police no one is protected. Bystanders are caught in the cross fire between police and criminals, criminals who get wounded and or killed by police and police officers who get wounded and or killed by criminals. Often gang members shoot at the rival members creating dramas for the media who cannot wait to put them in the headlines of their newspapers. America has it all; it is car theft capital of the World, loiterers, strutters, swiggers, extorters, pickpocketers, vandalizers, graffiti artists, bribers, smugglers, money launderers, kidnappers, human traffickers, stalkers, computers and machinery thieves, sex offenders, child molesters, rioting prisoners, arsonists, husbands killing wives and children, mothers drowning their own kids, baby-sitters who abuse babies, house keepers who get raped, and presidents are war criminals who must go on trial for crime against humanity but fall short of being punished due to the International, bureaucratic, and double standards injustice shadowing the World of today. America, today, is a sick society (just opposite to what Ronald Reagan said when he said "Americans are not living in a sick society" and I wonder if what he said is true, then, why he said that in the first place) in which family values are vanishing, Catholic priests who molest children, church goers repeat same things over and over with no conclusion at the end, priests who have mastered their ability to tediously preech and sermon from the Bible over years by repeating thousands of times just to get the vulnerable audience bored who are not immune anymore against the sermons. To all these social problems existing in the American society one must add the, so to speak, church crime. As many know lots of churches have been in the practice of fooling its' members not only by collecting money but thru their magical power of healing the sick who gets cured suddenly out of nowhere by having some of the associates pretend like a sick with a long time decease and then at the mercy of Christ the sick suddenly gets cured or by using devices such as an earphone in the priest's ears who is informed of a sick newcomer's arrival thru another church associate who communicates with the priest using a one way radio unknown to the church members. Later on this deceptive priest is able to find the sick among the members and out of nowhere heals the sick by virtue of his own blessing. This miracle of church power reminds me of some of the deceptive miracle and extraordinary powers many fakirs of India claim to have such as subduing a snake whose fangs have already been extracted. In America wrenching methods of public deception takes different forms. Ads in the papers advertised by companies and individuals containing subjects such as dating services, finding jobs, work from homes, marketing, how to get rich in just few days or weeks, etc. The story of how to become a millionaire is just an example in which the advertiser asks for only $1. for showing the subscriber on how to become a millionaire. It happened that about one million people responded to his ad, each by sending him $ 1. When the man collected the one million dollars, that was his claim and way to prove to the public about how to become a millionaire. Or the con man who claimed to be a doctor without possessing a M.D. license beat the system by working in a hospital as a doctor for while, seeing patients, collecting large amount of money and at last when caught he ridiculed the system. He very well shed the light on the fact that unimaginable can happen in America known as land of laws (at least as Bill Clinton put it). But laws are just words in the books, unless they are enforced equally to everyone indiscriminately. And this is where America falls short of proving it. In the land of justice, justice is raped when O.J. Simps got away with murdering two innocent people; Bill Clinton and Janet Reno the responsible murderers of eighty six men, woman, and children in Waco, Texas along with the criminal F.B.I. agents got away with justice. What a slap in the face of justice! If the hostages in Waco were alive and asked which one they would prefer: to remain hostage or to be blown up by the gas explosion perpetrated by F.B.I. agents, would they not choose the first option over the latter? Did Bill Clinton and his Attorney General Janet Reno ever go on trial? Where is implementation of justice in the system? This is the land where the shameful highway patrol in Florida used to ambush on young women, taking them behind trees by force and rape them; all in the name of traffic violations, or the officer who raped and murdered the young woman in San Diego! And what happened to the war criminal George W. Bush for exterminating thousands of innocent civilians of Afghanistan and Iraq by dropping bombs over them? American soldiers' crime in both those two countries is leaving the stigma of shame on the fans of human rights believers and activists. All this American crime in the name of fighting terror; that terror is created by the Americans and the real terrorist is the American Government. There is a very obvious similarity between the killing and genocide committed by the American soldiers in Afghanistan and especially in Iraq on one hand and the atrocity and terrorism perpetrated by the Israelis soldiers in Palestine. How dare the American soldiers force themselves thousands of miles into Iraq dropping bombs over innocent people, holding them at gun point, handcuffing them, blind folding them, terrorizing them, dragging them, holding them thirsty, hungry, frightened, tortured, pulling them out of their homes, destroying their homes, slaughtering them in different ways including firing squad, raping women, end even children, burying them in mass graves like they did to innocent Vietnamese women and children in the trench. What is truly sickening is that after all this they claim to be fighting against terrorism; the truth is just the opposite. We have currently for sure three big terrorist governments, one is the U.S. Government and the other is its' puppet Israel and the Third one is the Government of Mullas in Iran. This is the real America. They may fool the American people once or twice but the truth will eventually come out, just as Abraham Lincoln said: "you may fool people once, you may fool them twice, but you cannot fool them forever".

America is supposed to be a democratic country. Before the Iraq war began for the second time, once by George Bush senior (also a war criminal) and the second time by George Bush junior in March of 2003, millions of people sent their opposition to the war to White House thru e-mail, fax, phone calls, and mail. I was one of them.I said no, Desmond Tutu of South Africa said no, Dalai Lama of Tibet said no, United Nation said no, millions of human beings around the World including millions of Americans and human rights activists said no. The nature of the beast George Bush prevailed his wisdom and the criminal Congress and its' blood thirsty president could no longer wait for the mass murder in Iraq. Bush is just as criminal as Saddam Hussein. His father committed same crime some thirteen years ago. The final conclusion is the thousands of lives lost apparently for the sake of ousting and or capturing one dictator called Saddam Hussein or another perpetrator called Osama Ben Laden. But, if Ben laden and Hussein are dictators and murderers because of killing innocent people, then, so is George Bush who did same crime. Crime is crime. There is no difference whether people get killed by Hussein's chemicals or American air raids. Moreover, Iraqis would be happier under Hussein's savage regime than to die by American bombs, after all everybody's life is precious. The same analogy holds true about Afghanistan where Taliban's cruel regime is preferred than the large, miserable exodus carrying all kinds of calamity for the Afghan people as well as dying in bombardment.

September 11, 2001 occurrence was a very lucid and direct reflection of U.S.A. crime in many countries around the World for many years especially Saudi Arabia which has been used like a base to quench American masters' greed and urge to shed blood, exploiting small countries by abusing their weak governments. In 1952 The American Government made its' big blunder of regime change in Iran where Dr. Mohammad Mossaghegh got replaced by a dictator called Mohammad Reza Pahlavi to rule for decades to come. It appeared that for all those years that the Shaw was in power Americans living in Iran were having a luxurious life, getting paid high salary from Iran's Government, selling weapons to Iran, getting cheap oil, and trading in many different forms. The profits pouring into U.S.A. from Iran could not last for ever. In 1979 things changed for Americans as the regime in Iran was replaced. The loss U.S.A. has been taking since then is much greater than the profits they gained and enjoyed during dictatorship of Shaw of Iran. On the top of that the bitter memories of the American conspiracy to topple Dr. Mossaghegh has never gone from the mind of those Iranians who are aware of such dirty American interference. Iranians still carry hostility towards the U.S. Government for that satanic plot.

America what a country!

The richest depressed country in the World suffers from its' biggest social dilemmas; first crime and then homelessness. It was estimated that there are between two to three million homeless Americans in the country. When we talk about homelessness we talk about all the consequences of this sick social phenomenon. When one is homeless not only he does not have a roof to sleep under but also he suffers both physically and psycho -logically from despair, no future, no food, no clothes, no shower, no health, no medicine, no money, no music, no car, no telephone, no relative who can be accessible, no sexual contact and no relationship.. Sanitary is a joke for a homeless who is at the bottom of his life. Whatever he receives is temporary. His shelter is either the carton box where he or she sleeps or the tacky sleeping bag. That's all he has whether it shines or rains, hot or cold, foggy or snowy, day or night. These people pass by thousands of ordinary people everyday in their short and miserable life, but all they can do is to ask for help on a continuos basis. Sometimes a grocery cart is added to their luxury. It was estimated that about one third of the homeless population in U.S.A. are drug and alcohol addicted, another one third mentally sick, and the other third people are ordinary people but due to different factors they became homeless. In the richest country where there are more than two million millionaires and the top government officials, senators, representatives of the house, local councilmen and women and judges get raise in their already high salary, two to three million Americans are deprived from the minimum living standards which is the subject of those who live under poverty line. A homeless who suffers from lack of health care also suffers from lack of dental and vision care. The bottom line is that a homeless not only is a human who does not have a home but does not have anything. And if this happens in Africa, it would be considered typical. But when it happens in America, it is a big slap in the face of the social system. In the land run by capitalism only one commodity rules: money. If one has money, and lots of it, he is ok, if not he is doomed. In the hierarchy of human needs a homeless gets only the first two easy; air and water. The best attention they can get from the Government is when the coroner examines his body to find out the cause of death. Seasons have no meaning in the mind of a homeless. When he looks at flowers in Spring time, he probably wishes they could be edible. He probably imagines a twenty five cent coin when he notices a hole in his shoes or dreams about food in his dreams. Hunger is a very strong drive, no one is immune when it strikes. One has to have food to survive. Survival in America does not come handy. Every year a great number of homeless Americans die because of the causes related to their conditions of living. America will never sleep in peace as long as there is crime and homelessness.

America what a country!

The richest country refuses to provide all it's citizens with health insurance, dental and vision insurance, something which even Communist countries provide but not U.S.A. It is a shame because as the country is wealthy it is expected that more social service goes to it's people than less fortunate countries. But as we see it is just the opposite.

America has the most expensive health care system in the World. The premium to pay to have insurance can exceed income of many people who live on the nominal income they earn. There are millions of families who survive on $200. a month while buying health insurance for the whole family can cost over eight hundred dollars a month. Talk is cheap especially when it comes from politicians. I remember when Bill Clinton was holding the governor's position and at the same time he was preparing himself to run for presidency he eagerly reiterated his talkativeness by giving all those lectures about different subjects including social security and health insurance. But as nature of politics necessitates lie comes out very handy for government officials. They know they can get away with it later. A promise is just a promise and as long as it is not threatened by enforcement, it is O.K. It is O.K. from their perspective and not the public who want to see the promise to be committed and backed up by achievement. Because the promise is made unilaterally, therefore, it appears that he who makes the statement also has the right to waive it! And this is the story of all those who are in the business of deceiving the public and it is not limited to U.S. Even if it may be the Congress which vetoes such bills, people see the president as responsible. But people get hurt anyway regardless of who does it at top level. If it is the future president who promises, and the congress fails to follow them up, then, the first one (the promiser) is a liar and the second one (the congress) is negligent.A bill taken to Congress by a president wishing to pass it is either good for the American people or bad. If bad, it should have not been created in the first place. If it is good, then.it should be pessed by Congress.

The health insurance plight is still where it used to be with no hope of positive result in near future. Millions in the private sectors cannot afford to pay for health insurance. The Government has to jump in to subsidize it at least for those who have a limited income. George Bush the Junior, the number 2 war criminal after his father has wasted billions of dollars in Afghanistan and Iraq. He also requested the congress eighty seven billion dollars to reconstruct Iraq which was demolished and turned into a rubble by order of his administration and approval of the congress. If it is not broke, why fix it? They destroyed the country, now they want to build it, how intelligent! A fraction of this massive budget could go for health insurance instead of creating a war in the first place and then clean up the mess. The skyrocketing cost of surgery, hospitalization, and drugs can eat up most of the third class people's income who cannot afford the premiums, forcing them to the streets and turn them into homeless. Considering the fact that U.S. population is now more than any other time in the short history of the nation, the American society is among some of the nations not providing health insurance for it's citizens. Only idiots may brag about such a vacuum.

America what a country!

Country of blue jeans, books and lots of it, cars as many as one wishes, energy waste as much as one third of the energy in the World is used in U.S.A., land of plastic and garbage, land of paper work and paper waste, land of formalities, obesity, artificial food, hormones, diabetes, heart attack, too much food more than one can take, land of measures such as gallons, inches, pounds, foot, yard, and mile versus litre, centimeter, kilos, meter, and kilometer. Land of home grown vegetables, green house effect, too much wastes, and dumps, fast growing 24 hour open supermarket, and gas stations, land of too many malls and mall goers, land of overspending, land of money and cloths where they are no longer worn for necessity; in the past necessity was mother of inventions, now they invent to create necessity. Land of sneakers and jeans, land of biggest and most expensive weapons and their operations, accommodations, all kinds of weapons of mass destruction, land of first tested atomic bomb, the land which dropped the first atomic bomb, burning to death and turning into smoke in seconds tens of thousands of Japanese, land of paper cups and plates, land of coca cola and other harmful sodas where millions are negatively affected by them so that doctors won't be out of job, where there are always enough law suits to keep lawyers busy, where one does not have to seek assistance from lawyers by chasing them but they seek you and find you and come to you, after all ripping off and creating law suits is as common as police officers ripping off the public by giving them tickets to make money for corporate America. This is land of plenty of everything, plenty of suicide, the victims and victimizers, tax and tax payer, the mentally sick and psychologists, franchisees and franchisors, patients and physicians, the cheaters and the cheated, land of laws and law breakers, in essence, land of beauty and beast!

America what a country!

Where higher education not only ls not free at the mercy of capitalism!, but is the most expensive in the World. Universities are practically buisinesses which pull in hundreds of millions of dollars every year from tuition.

Internet graduating is the latest phenomenon in this money hungry society. Holding big parties on college campuses at different times of the year for different excuses is just one way of generating revenue; there has to be a connection between the university and the venders. Another way is to turn sport into business like The American Football games, for example, held at U.C.L.A. By the time a medical college student graduates, he has paid more than two hundred thousand dollars for tuition, books, and etc. There are millions of young Americans who just cannot afford to pay for all these costs. There are loans and grants, but not everybody is eligible to receive them. In the case of loan many are not lucky enough to find a job six months after graduation in order to be able to start paying the loan back with high interest rate. As the capitalism system dictates there is no guaranty of getting a job after finishing college and on the top of that competition for job is fierce. Foreigners pay over all, two and a half times more for tuition than a resident does. The bottom line is that it all boils down to money! One does not have to work on his thesis, but just pay some nominal money to some institutions who would provide you with a thesis about the subject you asked for. As easy as that. How wonderful!

America what a country!

It is said that America is made of people from other nations, the immigrants, primarily. Immigrants who came here in search of better life, but many have seen their lives turning upside down; joblessness, suicide, victims of crime, many people who lost their lives in the hands of Americans! The Mexican mother who lost her daughter when crossing street and caught in the cross fire of gang members, Japanese college students who were robbed and shot to death, German visitors whose car was stolen and they themselves were shot to death, the car salesman who was held at gun point and shaken to death, the guard who got both robbed and killed, the man who was shot to death over parking space, and cases of forty thousand crime victims who vanish every year in this country because the system does not function well. It is not unusual to know that in the hodge podge transition of the applicants for residency from one department to another within the immigration organization, documents get shuffled and lost. Sometimes one's Green Card is sent to the wrong person and if one waits for the I.N.S. to inform him and or fix the problem, he is whistling in the wind! Waiting in the long lines,too much paper work and red tape go hand in hand when it comes to Immigration Department. When the system malfunctions, the Government officials, as if they have been trained to have the answer handy, say" well, the system is not perfect". Therefore, every time something goes wrong one may expect to hear that response. In the land of lines, lines in the banks, post office, I.N.S., city municipalities, counties, federal buildings, D.M.V.., courts, police stations, sherif's department, etc. one may run out of patience. In the land claimed to be a free society and democratic in which people are welcomed to have the right to choose any ideology including political, foreigners, in a sneaky way, are excluded from the above mentioned right to democracy. This shameful and notorious double standard policy is even explicitly questioned in the questionnaire of the applicants applying for residency and citizenship where they are asked if they believe in Communism. And obviously the applicant's request will be rejected upon his indulgence of such an ideology. Since this anti -democracy and immoral policy is 180 degrees in opposition direction to what the Government claims, the Government tends to have it hidden in and limited to I.N.S. papers. One cannot defend human rights (believing in any political ideology is one of them) on one hand and violate human rights on the other, just as The American Government has done to prisoners in the Abughraib Prison in Iraq and the Guantanamo Prison in

Cuba. Therefore, in light of such inference having respect for people's freedom of political ideology on one hand and having them deprived from it on the I.N.S. forms as a condition to adopt them for permanent residency and or citizenship is a contradiction which the Government utilizes on these easy targets(the foreigners). After September 11, 2001 the manipulator and real criminal of the justice system John Ashcroft The Attorney General of the Justice System came up with the humiliating and truly degrading law of having arrested anybody suspicious and also listening to their conversations by eaves dropping and authorizing police officers to search anybody anywhere anytime for no reason, and stopping people under any circumstances they wish, all in the name of national security. This is totally contrary to the foundation based which this country was established in the first place. If John Ashcroft were smart, he would have exterminated crime in this country which has rooted for over a century. Holding human beings without due process, invading their privacy, intruding into their vehicles, snatching, arresting and detaining innocent people in Guantanamo Bay, fabricating charges against them, depriving them from having access to lawyers, family members, friends and committing other violations of human rights is part of the crime the ruthless George

Bush Administration is perpetrating. This is all immoral, illegal, and against religion criteria and humanity. This is 180 degrees deviation from the right way and from what our Government is screaming out loud clubbing the World that America is land of justice, democracy, freedom, defense of human rights, and respect for human rights, what big words!. America is dropping crocodile's tears! When finally under international pressure the legitimacy of holding detainees in the Guantanamo Bay was disputed by lawyers with the court, the corrupt court system concluded that "lower courts had found that the American civilian court system did not have authority to hear the men's complaints about their treatment"; and it goes on:" The United States has created a prison on Guantanamo Bay that operates entirely outside the law,"lawyers for British and Australian detainees argued in asking the high court to take the case. Here is one reason why we really believe George Bush's Administration and his Attorney General John Ashcroft are the real criminals, anti-American (if there is such a thing), anti-constitution and in one word terrorists. The same lawyers arguing for the release of the detainees continue" Within the walls of this prison, foreign nationals may be held indefinitely, without charges or evidence of wrongdoing, without access to family, friends or legal counsel, and with no opportunity to establish their innocence," they maintained!

America what a country!

Where many innocent humans go to jail, many truly criminals walk out free, many Government officials break the rules and get away at the mercy of the criminal "Uncle Sam", where for the past half a century America has had a very long dossier of supporting countries which suppress their own citizens, ignore human rights adopted by U.N., beat up their own citizens, torture and imprison their political opponents, create an atmosphere of intimidation, creating stifling political conditions, perishing people, kidnapping them, confiscating their tangible and intangible goods, disappearing dissidents like magicians do to their instruments of magic; in essence depriving people from their own country and from all or almost all the standards of living which every human being deserves to have. For the past fifty years the World has witnessed American hypocrisy and cruelty in El Salvador, Guatemala, Columbia, Panama, Iran, Africa, Chile, Argentine, Egypt, Saudi Arabia, Turkey, etc. As long as the unelected governments of those countries have a tight friendly relationship with the U.S. Government the American Government has no problem to rationalize illegality of those illegitimate regimes. But if any of those countries leader turns his back on the U.S. Government, the American Government is willing to stab him in the back and to destabilize that country. In the case of Noriega of Panama it was the criminal U.S. Government which tackled him with drugs and weapons in the first place. A beast is a beast, no matter what, no matter where. The U.S. Government is dropping crocodile's tears over The September 11, 2001 event when the American army got involved in killing thousands of Afghan civilians by dropping bombs over them. Why innocent people of Afghanistan had to be frightened to death and blown up? It was the transparent and guaranteed dirty foreign policy demonstrating the vast dimension of U.S. atrocity and tyranny. We have witnessed this in Iraq where thousands lost their lives all in the name of capturing one person, Saddam Hussein. Even after capturing him and months after finding no sign of weapons of mass destruction The U.S. Army continued it's occupancy of Iraq by staying there and accommodating their hand picked government. If they were honest, they would have pulled out after Saddam was captured. At the end, the truth about weapons of mass destruction turned out to be the B-52 Bombers of the U.S. Army, as put by Ralph Nader, (the presidential candidate for the year 2000 and 2004), over the already suppressed and oppressed people once by Saddam Hussein and now by the terrorist George Bush Administration. What was supposed to be liberation gave way to occupation. Stealing Iraq's oil and funneling it to another terrorist government such as Israel which has been in the business of terrorizing Palestinians for almost four decades is another international crime America is associated with.

The most powerful capitalist state follows the path of it's most feared enemy, the Communist Soviet Union, now called Russia, of Stalin and Brezhnev by eaves dropping, intimidating opponents, arresting anybody anytime for any excuse, using the embedded media (especially CNN and Fox news), keeping people in prisons illegally. These are exactly what used to happen in the Soviet Union in the past. But this is America today five years into the 21st Century they are wire tapping and eaves dropping! What a freedom!

America what a country!

Where the wealthiest government has given its poorest attention and respect for humans' life, to its army where hundreds of thousands of American soldiers against their desire are deployed to other countries like Germany, Japan,

South Korea for decades and recently Afghanistan and Iraq by stationing them in those countries, all in the name of security and peace while there is a very obvious lack of safety and security and peace inside the American society. How can the country which has failed to provide security and safety for its own citizens inside the country establish safety and security in other countries? It was not the soldiers' choice in the first place to be far from home and in some cases the duration of nostalgia has lingered for years for those soldiers. Many of them after living abroad and surviving the war for years, lost their lives inside U.S. cities when they returned to their homeland. Frankly, soldiers' lives does not mean anything to the Government, otherwise, they would not be sent to places against their will, places where they lost their lives unjustifiably because of the bully Government, places like Afghanistan, Iraq, Vietnam, Korea. None of these countries attacked America to give it a reason for invasion. If U.S. were invaded by any of those Governments, sending troops to the battlefield could be justified. In the Iraq War an unwise and, indeed, mad decision made in the congress which discredited U.S.A. before the World and U.N., was rushed in to wage war against humanity creating exodus of few millions of some of the neediest people, dislodging and rambling them to all directions for the fear of the American weapons of mass destruction. A sense of madness, lack of humanity and love for genocide is apparent here. So far, as this episode is written, roughly, about over one thousand American soldiers have died in Iraq only. The war is still taking its toll on both sides. To the White House it is like one thousand pigs have been slaughtered. Seems like this number is not high enough to convince the war chasing authorities of Washington to withdraw the forces to prevent more disaster. Where wisdom cannot be justified, crime is moralized to do act of evil. When one does wrong, no news should be good news for the perpetrator. This is the story of the American soldiers, they lost their lives in vain in Korean War, Vietnam War, in Afghanistan, and in Iraq. The only people who may cry over the soldiers' dead bodies and carry the pain of such sorrow is their family members and not the cruel and callous U.S. Government. Today if Cuba which is considered an enemy of U.S. bowes to The American Government, no longer it is considered hostile. Therefore, friendship or hostility of a nation is not in the nature of those countries but relative to the relation they have with U.S. and to what degree they can satisfy the massive greed of this monster. If they bend over, the green light may go on, but if they bend backward, a red flag may go up. This is precisely how the White House justifies its relationship with other countries; a childish behavior based on emotion and not logic, getting and not giving, force, not understanding, taking advantage, not helping, exploitation and not a fair and sound relation. For fifty years The United States Government has been hostile towards N. Korea, about 40 years towards Cuba, 25 years towards Iran. In case of Vietnam the thing is that the U.S. was defeated otherwise same hostile attitude would have been chosen and used. I laugh at the simplicity of those Americans who give their consent and pride to the posters and placards saying "support pur troops"or " God bless America," and or" one nation under God". If there is a God, why would that God favor only Americans versus their enemies ? Isn't this what the enemy also wishes for their own? Therefore, here we have a confused God who is rocking between whom to favor: a criminal like Bush dropping bombs on people or people of Iraq and Afghanistan who are the victims of his despotism and atrocity. How naive are those who believe or are taking their chance that God would bless them despite the massacre their government does to other nations. And if their wish could come true and God would have listened to them, why over one thousand American soldiers have died against their will in the occupied land of Iraq ? Hence, we have to come to the inference that either prayers on posters do not get God's attention maybe they are not big enough for God to see them, or are not highly visible due to poor locations,(don't forget" location, location, location) or if God favors only one particular nation, that God has to be a cruel and discriminating one, and who would believe in such a God?

America is where the Government wants the World to believe how peaceful and peace lover Americans are. And if being peaceful on one hand, and on the other hand, having the most massive stock of arsenals in the World are in contradiction to each other, then, definitely something is wrong with this nation. It is so for the obvious reason that about 55% of the World military budget is designated to the, so to speak, peace loving Government of the United States of America!, In other words, the rest of the World has taken only 45% of the military budget combined and yet there are not even covering half of the whole military expenses. The U.S. military budget is about $400,000,000,000, Russia $ 60,000,000,000, China $ 50,000,000,000. In other words, U.S. military budget counts 8 times more than that of China, the most populated nation. I call this a very fair utopia in Hell, the Utopia they have made for themselves and the hell for the rest of the World! And also it is here that ninety five percent of the private wealth is possessed by only five percent of the corrupt, rich class, in other words, five percent of the population has been sucking up blood from the majority of the country residents for the past half of a century. This is the country where by virtue of wealth, power, and influence The United Nations Organization found its home. It was a big blunder to have agreed to such a decision when nations got together to find a future home. The reason is very clear: the influence U.S. plays as the host over nations overpowering smaller and weaker countries by wagging it's tail, bragging its' power and wealth on them, sometimes thru intimidation by threat of depriving them from loans, grants, trading, selling weapons or rejecting their proposals, and etc. And the worst humiliating one is when the American Government refuses to give visa to some of the U.N. member representatives to attend the Security Council. That is a very double standard, discriminating, and hostile act. It is simply wrong to base U.N. in a country like here where some of the most crucial decisions about the World are made. For the purpose of fairness the United Nations must move to a, so to speak, Third World country or at least to an impartial and civilized country such as Switzerland, Austria, Denmark, or Scandinavia. Those who came up with plans, rules, regulations, and resolutions had good intentions but were not smart enough to adopt an effective enforcing policy in case one member does not obey the unanimous decision won by the Security Council or does not follow thru step by step or does not get authorization to carry out the appropriate policy, then, that member country must be subject to more sever punishment than just sanctions and or condemnation. Hence, if those not so genius members had thought about the consequence of such an ill policy, today both Israel and U.S. would have been subject to wrenching punishment policy other than just condemnation. Israel has been condemned frequently and U.S. attacked Iraq two times, Afghanistan once, and interfered in internal affairs of many countries in the second half of the twentieth Century. These two aggressive Governments are way overqualified to get sanctions and be thrown out of U.N. For the past few decades U.N. warned and condemned Israel for aggression and human rights violations against Palestinians. Since this is as far as it can go, Israel has learned not to be concerned about the crime and genocide it has been doing to the real settlers of Palestine. In the case of the American Government, we all know how disgraceful it was for the country when it was discredited by U.N. when it launched its war machines against Iraq in March of 2003. Michael Moore the movie director of "Fahrenheit 9/11 " was thinking what I was thinking when at the Award winning ceremony he said "shame on you Mr. Bush, shame " as an objection to the outset of the war on Iraq. Letters from different parts of The World, many from celebrities including some from prominent individuals from the American people and some other countries went to Hague, Netherlands requesting George Bush to be put on trial as a war criminal against humanity. It appears that the decision making panel in Hague is either corrupt or somehow disable to bring Bush to justice by placing him in the same booth in Nuremberg where at the end of World War 2 the war criminals of the Nazi Germany were put on trial and later executed. This is self explanatory and speaks for itself how fragile are even those organizations claiming to be supporting and enforcing justice and human rights around the World. If there were such a thing as justice and international police force, we would have seen in the Hague International Court faces like George W. Bush the Texan cowboy warmonger, Donald Rumsfield the Secretary of war, Dick Cheney the oil thief, and Powell the yes man of the corrupt Government, The vicious circle. The final conclusion leads us to the fact that, as mentioned at the beginning of this book, justice is only for the poor and weak, it has been like that so far and will be that way for centuries to come.

America what a country!

Land of too many cars, too many radio and t.v. stations, too many books all kinds including junk books, where even prostitutes write books, too much paper waste, too many atomic bombs, too many weapons but not enough sympathizers, too many guns but not enough opponents, too much protein consumption but not enough vegetarians, too much embezzlement but not enough enforcement, too much gray area (an immoral unjustifiable way to moralize one's action while knowing it is wrong) but not enough honesty, too many flakes but not enough straightforwardness, too much cutting trees but not enough futurism, too many car accidents and too much death toll, too many drunk drivers and substance users, too many victims of those accidents, where when in an emergency situation one goes to hospital the first thing they do is to make sure the patient has health insurance and or money or somehow a kind of warranty of financial security before being admitted, where this red tape may play the roll of life or death in patients, where paperwork has priority over one's life in hospitals, where the Government claims in reducing paperwork while reality says something else. In the land of freedom the homeless is free to sleep in a box on the streets in cold winter time because that is the only choice he has, where in New York City police officers watch over drivers' shoulders lest they are not buckled up after all the already fat Police Department is not acting fat enough with millions of dollars they have gained already; they still need to come up with any kind of laws by which they can make more money, why not ripping off the public,! the easy target? As if people don't know how to protect themselves and only the Government can be the right doctor to prescribe a prescription for the citizens, telling them how to take care of themselves and determine their life style for them.. If this is a free country, why are people not free whether to buckle up or not, to wear helmet or not ? They are saying that jury duty is every American's duty. In other words, the Government would penalize those who refuse; and this is exactly registered in the jury duty forms sent to people. My question is; does this not lead us to the reality that if we live in a free and democratic society, then, why are we not free to decide for ourselves whether to serve as a juror or not? Also imagine the consequence of such a pressure and threat when attending the court.A person who is not voluntarily willing to participate as a juror, can he or she be an impartial judge? Is it not possible that one who serves as a juror against his will may take revenge by giving a bad judgment about the defendants whose trial outcome depends on such jurors? And if jury duty is everybody's duty, why the Government makes discrimination by excluding doctors, lawyers and some other segments of the society to serve as such? What is good for the goose is good for the gander. Here in California the State Government is telling people in the driver's license book that driving in California is a priviledge and not a right. If that's so, then, what if people don't drive here in this state, who would? Would that be only a bunch of the Government officials who would have the right to drive, which in this case, are they separated and different from the rest of the society to have the right to drive in the State but not the citizens? Is the country not for the people who live in it ? I would suggest that the Government be brave enough to take away this priviledge from people, the real owners of the country, so that we see who will remain to use roads in the State. And if this is a privilege, then, who has the right to drive in freeways in California? Those very genius lawyers and congressmen and women and or council men and women whoever invented such a bright invention were not smart enough to think of the consequence of such an insertion into a government document. Again here the Government is dropping crocodile tears by saying to people that they can drive, and on the other hand it is telling the citizens that it is doing them a favor. What a favor! Was it not we the people who have elected our representatives to be our agents in the Government cabinets to do the best for us? Does the country not belong to us the people ? So, we citizens of the United States of America put some of us to run our government to tell us that we do not have the right to drive in our own state, but, if we do, we should consider it as a favor the master is doing to his slaves.I always thought that in a free democratic society the country is run for people and by people. Does the constitution not start with " we the people."...?

In the land of too many magazines, newspapers, V.C.R., T.V. sets, game machines, in this land all the ways end up in one direction, money. Everything everybody ever does is crystalized in money; that's the utopia! Even psychology magazines encourage the society to do every thing for money. They are too shy to include crime as part of the package in their propaganda, but one can conclude it's inclusion. This is the land where if the customs officer does not like someone for whatever the reason, he does not mind to throw your documents towards you instead of handling it and if you protest by trying to take the case to the manager, the manager hides himself in the back room like he is not available. And if you persist in standing for your rights, they threaten you by calling a security guard; they don't care how rightful you are. Once a Government clerk has got the job he or she has got on the horse and guides it in the direction he or she wishes. This is how all government jobs are handled. They tell the public that the public is supposed to get courtesy services from any government office, but the truth proves deferent. There are horror stories about people who went to police stations for help but they were terrorized, arrested, and even jailed. In a city like Los Angeles if one needs help by calling 911, he must expect a police officer to show up not sooner than forty minutes later. When somebody calls 911 in an emergency the clerk asks you the victim or whoever the caller is so many questions that in many cases by the time a police officer arrives at the scene either the criminal has got away or the bloody caller has passed away. This happens often. Such is the fate of everyone who lives in a metropolitan area. The law of jungle dominates.

America what a country!

This is the country where in a small claim court the judge may ask you (say plaintiff) to hand her your documents and you happened to have the original papers. Upon termination of the court she would tell you that she needs to look at them later to make her decision. Upon losing the case you may want to appeal the case to a higher court. You find out that you left your documents with the judge. When you ask for it they tell you that she is gone and you have to write to her. You do so and are told that they lost your paper.you lose the case at the mercy of the sloppy, disorganized and irresponsible system! Also it is here that when they take you to jail on charge of unproved charge, get you naked and later shuffle and sandwich you with the rest of the herd like the society does to chickens in a cruel way and after few days of being in jail innocently, even despite the defendant drops off the case against you the scandalous system does not leave you alone. They make you go to the court once a month for 4 months and all you see is that your, so to speak, defense lawyer (picked by court) who whispers in the judge's ears and then tells you go and come back another month without telling you about your rights and that what the conversation was between your defense lawyer and the judge. When you mention to your court -picked lawyer that the defendant had a gun illegally and that you are willing to prove it, your own lawyer just does not care nor does the system gives it a damn. This is the country where court judges ignore the hippocratic oath they were taught at school to be impartial and make a fair judgment based on evidences and not emotions, gender, nationality, and other double standards which are very common here in this country. Judges who may give someone judgment because the judge is a female, and so is the plaintiff or defendant who would get the favor, and if that person shows some emotions and in the meantime is a white American, he or she is almost guaranteed to win the case despite the fact the other party who may be a foreigner may have an upper hand in proving the case. In America, generally speaking, plaintiffs are in trouble as long as getting a fair trial. The writer has witnessed such unjust cases numerously. Even when the defendant was properly served and present in the court which means he or she was served otherwise would not be there in the first place, the sherif (the uniformed person in the courtroom) would still give the plaintiff hard times for nothing by asking the plaintiff if he served the defendant and that where the proof is. The system is simply deficient. If the defendant is attending the courtroom, why is the plaintiff asked whether he served the defendant? How could the defendant not be notified on one hand and also be present in the court without being served ? This is for sure a sign showing how sick the court system is and that they cannot solve this very simple social defect. Dismissal of cases to the benefit of defendant is much more common than running for and winning presidency by cheating on people of Florida in the election year of 2000 committed by the war criminal George Bush with the help of his brother being governor of Florida to make sure the cheating process goes smooth and their father another criminal Bush as ex-president to influence the Republican political party and activities to benefit his would-be president. America is where those sheriffs working in court houses and rooms are basically rude and aggressive. Their job lacks intelligence, after all the simple acts they perform can be done by any elementary school kid. Their presence is practically useless. A pre-taped cassette player can do what they preach in the courtrooms and the paper exchange can be achieved easily between the judge, plaintiff and defendant. This is the society where moral turpitude at all levels from lowest position to president of The United States of America and from private sector to different Government Departments is highly prevalent. A high society bearing its own side effects of all kinds of wrongdoing and cover up. Let's not forget about another bogus institution called American Arbitration. This is an organization commonly involved in Real Estate issues, ripping off plaintiffs for several hundred dollars even before the trial begins. Often the mediator who apparently works voluntarily (hungry for fame and publicity) makes a bad judgment just as the court judges do; the result is that one party (usually the plaintiff) may lose the case unfairly plus several hundreds of dollars. For this reason I call the American Arbitration as American" Bullshittration". One may not know how bad it is until he or she tries it. The people who choose this institution as a mediator are those who know how time consuming and costly it is for the other party to take their grief to such an ominous organization.

While the Government pretends to sympathize towards consumption of some natural resources such as trees used for paper and the policy of cutting paperwork to save trees, the reality is that in spite of the recycling process of used paper, the paperwork associated with Government transactions has a long way to go to be considered real paperwork cut. One can look into many Government job application, social work related paperwork, D.M.V.., immigration, getting permit to establish a company, massive paperwork associated with trucking buisinesses, and so on. More than any other time in the history of this country paper is wasted today and trees are cut down. America at the mercy of its' vast natural sources is rich for quite a while otherwise by now it would have looked like a vast barren land the way people and Government misuse its' natural sources. America is the only country which the Government claims to be doing a favor to some nations like Afghanistan and Iraq by establishing liberation, justice, human rights, peace, prosperity, and many other words designed to deceive American laymen and women while the reality speaks of horrifying mistreatment of Iraqi detainees in such unethical, illegal, immoral, and torturous ways that being aware of all these crimes the American soldiers were doing to the Iraqi prisoners in the Abughraib Prison they treated them worse than one may treat animals; stack of naked men on top of each other, insulted, attacked sexually, chained up, blindfolded, and who knows what else. The extension of such murderous crimes has gone beyond imagination so that about 37 prisoners died under torture, not just locked up, but these people suffered so much from hunger, thirst, illness, beating, kicking, pushing, throwing, intimidation, holding them at gun point and other barbarous acts that they died. One has to understand how much one has to suffer under torture before dying. All these crimes have been ordered by the same army leaders who are savage enough to allow these to occur and then cowardly deny any wrong doing. This is the American justice system they club the World for. What a joke! America is where police officers are government's slaves, embedded media are comprised of yes men and yes women for government, land of child molesters, accusers and accused, where everybody sues everybody else, where government employees are simply underdogs of the Government and that's why one never hears any complaint from them (what a utopia!), where mushrooming colleges and universities race against each other for money. And finally this is the country where if one as a university student sheds light on some facts and or discloses his opinion in the local paper in opposition to those of that institution (teachers), they warn him and if that does not work, they get together like wild dogs to attack to bite off the victim's opinion. True freedom is a myth in America. As I said before it is a conditional one. Marlon Branden said once" people are free here but when they actually want to demonstrate it, they may end up like Martin Luther King".

In order for the World to live in peace.

The United Nations Organization must move out of U.S.A. to an impartial country. To to this the General Assembly needs to hold a session to decide about the details of this move and where to move to. Under no circumstances any U.N. member country has the right to attack another country without going thru U.N.. Regime change must happen by U.N. for good for the majority of the people of those countries. If this were done, Iraq and Afghanistan would not have turned into a rubble by Americans. The truth about finding weapons of mass destruction in Iraq turned out to be just a deceptive, obdurate, foreign policy of U.S. killing thousands of absolutely innocent humans, dilapidating cities, foraying oil, deprecating American reputation before the World and turning its back to U.N. and millions of philanthropists in so many different countries. It was simply a preemptive plan. The most important on behalf of the U.N. is to severly punish the violating government by using enforcement. After giving one time warning the U.N. must have the right to remove the leader of that country which refuses to follow U.N. proposal. For example, Israel's Ariel Sharon must be removed and put on trial on charge of overlooking U.N. warnings at times and doing crimes against Palestinians. Also George Bush must be removed from leadership for waging war without getting permission from U.N. and put on trial for war crimes. Another can be Iran's Khamenei and his vicious circle for human rights violations, and so on; the U.N. should take an immediate action for regime change in Iran by sending troops to bring the current barbarous primitive government of mullas down to it's knees and put the leaders on trial on charge of genocide for the past 25 years that U.N., U.S.A. and Europe have been dormant about their crimes. All the commercial fishing companies around the World must continue to be prohibited catching sea animals using several mile long nets known as drift fishing which sweep the Ocean floor without giving a chance to the fish to escape. Strict prohibition on catching certain sea animals such as dolphins and whales must be utilized. The Amazon jungle, the largest in the World must be preserved for its' animals (the savage hunting of monkeys is still taking their toll) including all the plants inhabited in it, meaning no more hunting its' animals and no more cutting trees for logging. Again UN. watchdog needs to keep eyes and enforcement to be used (in The state of Texas, U.S.A. barbarism is as common as monkey hunting in Amazon or Africa when hundreds of texans go after rattle snakes by pulling the poor animals out of their habitat just to use them for their skin and or eat them as gourmet food!). Another such inhumane act is what the spoilt, useless aristocrats of The British Monarchy commit when riding their horses using more than a dozen of barking dogs they chase foxes at a certain season. Or the ruthless murderous Canadians who club the seals to death in the Ocean every year at a certain season. Today mankind is as savage as hundreds and thousands of years ago, the only difference is he uses more sophisticated tools to do the crimes he is proud of. All countries must stop draining sewage into the Ocean, The largest water reservoir should be kept as clean as it used to be before mankind came aboard to pollute it. Bull fighting as well as dog fighting, rooster fighting and possibly some other animals fighting must be considered illegal and there must be enforcing punishment at least at local level in that country where the violation has taken place. No body has the right to trap, capture, and or kill elephants, giraffes, and rhinos. Hunting of any kind of animal, lions, tigers jaguars, etc., in general, must be prohibited by all people in every country. Trapping animals and using them in circus is barbarism and must stop. For fairness to be implemented either no country has the right to have atomic bomb or every country has the right to have if they wish. We do not have such a thing as civilized nation to have atomic bombs versus dangerous nations not to have it. Indeed, some of those who claim to be civilized are the ones who developed it, tested it, and dropped it on another nation. Hence U.N. should not fool itself, but to implement a unique policy for every country; fair is fair.

Governments such as Israel which ignored 1967 Security Council Resolution 242 must go back to the pact and give back the occupied land to its' original owners, Palestinians, as soon as possible. So far, U.N. has failed in this respects, as long as this game continues, U.N. has bogged down over its' mission of establishing peace in the region. Any other government such as U.S.A. supporting Israel must be punished by U.N. No nation must be allowed to exploitate another country by taking its resources or toppling or causing to topple those governments. Such decision to be made only by U.N. Therefore, the roll of U.N. will be extended. The U.N. Organization must see that elections in all countries are justly done and cheating has no place in a civilized world. By having correct and transparent information about what countries do, U.N. can make this World a better place to live. Of course there are so many other tasks which can be added to current agenda. Somehow and somewhere these tasks have to start and only time can show the success rate U.N. may have in implementing those policies.The items to be added to the United Nations agenda can be numerous. Perhaps the best fair way to see a relatively more peaceful and happy world is to share sources of wealth with other countries which suffer from lack of them or simply making The Earth Globe one big unit, one nation in which all the countries are family members. From this point on, all the efforts to be made towards the maximum welfare of residents on earth, human beings and animals. The last and final part is to strive to discover other planets as we humans still feel lonely here on earth all by ourselves, planets where we may find creatures who may show us how primitive our behavior is, after all, our behavior is a reflection of our thinking. So, we need to make corrections in the way we think: PEACE, PEACE, AND MORE PEACE.

If Osama Ben Laden was cause for about 2800 death in America, George Bush has murdered over 100,000 Iraqi civilians, innocent men, women and children. Therefore, at the ratio of 36 to 1 George Bush is 36 times more a muderous than his criminal counterpart. And who is that human being who is barbarious enough to humiliate humans of a certain nation over others?

The difference between Genghis Khan, the Mongolian conqueror who swept the Middle East some seven centuries ago and 21st Century Genghis Khan called George Bush, is the level of sofistacation of arms of how to radicate men, women and children in the least possible amount of time. Swords and horses which were the means used to kill individuals then, are now substituted with bombs and airplanes, the weapons of mass destruntion (exactly what the Bush's Administration accused Saddam Hussein of having) eliminating more people in a shorter period of time, an indication of continuation of barbarism at high dimentions in our time.

About the Author

At this writing and as this book goes to press in the next few months, the author in his 50's, father of 2, living in California dares to spill out things which have touched him for the past half of his lifetime. Being exposed to abundant injust ordeals since his college time throught his work experiences and in between, seeing and dealing with different class types of people at various settings in different environments, being victimized by society and malfunctioning of the system along with what seems to be a norm to an ordinary citizen due to brainstorming and brainwashing of everyday life as acknowledged and affected by embeded media, the author decided to shed light about what he recognizes as the social phenomena of a sick society. His first ordeal in college while studing for his Master's Degree began when he was vigorously and offensively confronted with the college Dean over author's political article in the town's newspaper and later on over another essay in the newsletter of the same university in 1978. The author blieves that everybody in his or her capacity should be part of this endeavor in the fact-finding process and not get fooled by promise of their gonvernment authorities.